George William Kitchin

The Life of Pope Pius II

as illustrated by Pinturicchio's Frescoes in the Piccolomini Library at Sienna

George William Kitchin

The Life of Pope Pius II
as illustrated by Pinturicchio's Frescoes in the Piccolomini Library at Sienna

ISBN/EAN: 9783743306318

Manufactured in Europe, USA, Canada, Australia, Japa

Cover: Foto ©ninafisch / pixelio.de

Manufactured and distributed by brebook publishing software (www.brebook.com)

George William Kitchin

The Life of Pope Pius II

CONTENTS.

	PAGE
INTRODUCTION	1

I. AENEAS . SILVIVS . PICCOLOMINEVS . NATVS . EST . PATRE SILVIO . MATRE . VICTORIA . XVIII . OCTOBR . MCCCCV . CORSIANI . IN . FVNDIS . GENTILITIIS . BASILEAM . AD . CONCILIVM . CONTENDENS . VI . TEMPESTATIS . IN . LIBYAM . PROPELLITVR 11

II. AENEAS . SILVIVS . A . BASILIENSI . CONCILIO . IN . VLTERIOREM . BRITANNIAM . ORATOR . AC . SCOTIAM . AD . REGEM . CALEXIVM . MISSVS . A . TEMPESTATE . IN . NOVERGIAM . PVLSVS . ET . PER . BRITANNIAM . REGIOS . SPECVLATORES . ELVDENS . BASILEAM . REVERTITVR . 19

III. HIC . AENEAS . A . FOELICE . V . ANTIPAPA . LEGATVS . AD . FEDERICVM . III . CAESAREM . MISSVS . LAVREA . CORONA . DONATVR . ET . INTER . AMICOS . EIVS . AC . SECRETARIVS . ANNVMERATVR . ET . PRAEFICITVR . 26

IV. AENEAS . A . FEDERICO . III . IMP . LEGATVS . AD . EVGENIVM . IIII . MISSVS . NON . SOLVM . EI . RECONCILIATVS . EST . SED . HIPODIACONVS . ET . SECRETARIVS . MOX . TERGESTINVS . DEINDE . SENEN . ANTISTES . CREATVS 32

V. AENEAS . FEDERICO . III . IMP . LEONORAM . SPONSAM . EXHIBET . ET . PVELLAE . LAVDIS . AC . REGVM . LVSITANORVM . COMPLECTITVR 41

VI. AENEAS . SENEN . ANTISTES . AD . CALISTVM . III . ORATOR . A . FEDERICO . IMP . III . MISSVS . PONT . AD . BELLVM . ASIATICVM . ARMAT . ET . PATRVM . PRINCIPVMQ . OMNIVM . ROGATIONE . CARD . EFFICITVR 44

PAGE

VII. CALISTO . MORTVO . AENEAS . CARDINALIS . SENEN . ACCLAMATIONE . PATRVM . APERTISQVE . SVFFRAGIIS . PONTIFEX . DELIGITVR . ET . PIVS . II . NOMINATVR . . 49

VIII. PIVS . II . PONT . MAX . A . LVDOVICO . MANTVANORVM . PRINCIPE . CLASSE . IN . NAVMACHIAE . SPECIEM . EXCEPTVS . VI . CALENDAS . IVNIAS . MANTVAM . AD . INDICTVM . DE . EXPEDITIONE . IN . TVRCOS . CONVENTVM . INGREDITVR 56

IX. PIVS . PONT . MAX . CATHARINAM . SENEN . OB . INNVMERA . EIVS . MIRACVLA . INTER . DIVAS . RETTVLIT . 60

X. PIVS . CVM . ANCON . EXPEDITIONE . IN . TVRCOS . ACCELERARET . EX . FEBRE . INTERIIT . CVIVS . ANIMAM . HEREMITA . CAMALDVLEN . IN . COELVM . EFFERRI . VIDIT . CORPVS . VERO . PATRVM . DECRETO . IN . VRBEM . REPORTATVM . EST 64

ÆNEAS SILVIUS BARTOLOMEUS PICCOLOMINI, POPE PIUS II.

INTRODUCTION.

THE noble houfe of the Piccolomini, which had been driven out of Siena and greatly impoverifhed by the political changes of the fourteenth century, was reftored to home and wealth by the influence of Pope Pius II. Among the moft notable of thofe Piccolomini who owed to him their renewed profperity was Francefco, whom he had made Cardinal, and who eventually became Pope as Pius III. His fenfe of gratitude and love of difplay have given us the fplendid chamber called the Piccolomini Library, and the ten frefcoes from the life of Pius II. which adorn the walls. For Francefco had much of that felf-efteem and vain-glory which, Dante tells us, characterized the Sienefe of his day :—

> " Ed io diffi al poeta : Or fu giammai
> Gente sì vana come la Sanefe ?
> Certo non la Francefca sì d'affai."
>   *Inferno*, xxix. 121.

It was fomething of this vanity which moved Cardinal Francefco to make this great family monument; he firft erected a rich chapel in his uncle's memory, againſt the left ſide of the nave of Siena Cathedral; and, this done, he ſhortly afterwards, in 1495, ſet to work on a Library by the ſide of the Chapel, in which he placed the valuable collection of books and MSS. bequeathed to him by his kinſman. Included among theſe were the originals of the Pontiff's own writings and memoirs. The whole of this collection has now diſappeared, and the chamber contains nothing but ſplendid ſervice-books, intended for the uſe of the Cathedral.

On this building the Cardinal determined to expend ſuch care and artiſtic ſkill as might make it a worthy monument of his patron, the reſtorer of his family, the benefactor and lover of Siena. Accordingly, he entruſted to a Sieneſe ſculptor, Lorenzo di Mariano (commonly called la Marrina), the entrance and outer decoration in marble; the bronze doors were deſigned and executed in 1497 by Antonio Ormanni; the interior wood-carving, done in 1496, was by the hand of Antonio Barili. And laſtly he called in Bernardino Pinturicchio, then in the height of his fame as a decorative artiſt, to adorn the walls and ceiling with freſco-work, ſo as to render the whole interior as rich and ſplendid as the vaineſt Sieneſe could deſire. The contract between the Cardinal and the painter, lately diſcovered at Siena by Signor Milaneſi, offers ſo many points of intereſt that it will not be amiſs if we here give a full tranſlation of the old Italian document:—

"In nomine Domini Amen. Be it known to all and
" every who ſhall read or ſee this preſent writing, that the
" moſt reverend lord Cardinal of Siena this day, June 29,

"1502, doth allot and contract out to M. Bernardino,
" called el Pentorichio, a painter of Perugia, the adorning
" of a Library in the Cathedral of Siena, on the fubfcribed
" conditions and agreements: viz. That during fuch time as
" this painting fhall be in progrefs, he fhall not undertake
" any other work of painting of any kind on panel or wall,
" whether in Siena or elfewhere, whereby the decorating
" of the faid Library may be deferred or delayed.

"Alfo, he fhall be held and bound to work at the vault-
" ing of the faid Library with thofe fantafies, colours, and
" divifions, which he fhall judge moft handfome, beautiful,
" and lively, in good, fine, agreeable colours, in the fafhion
" and with defigns now-a-days ftyled the 'Grotefque,' with
" the grounds varied, as fhall be deemed moft fair and
" handfome.

"Alfo, he fhall be held and bound, if in the centre of
" the vaulting there fhould be no coat of the arms of the
" moft reverend Cardinal depicted, there to draw fuch an
" one, rich and fine, of fuch dimenfion as fhall be deemed
" duly proportionate, in accordance with the size and lofti-
" nefs of the vaulting. And if fuch coat be already de-
" picted, then to paint it afrefh; and if it be of marble, to
" colour it as aforefaid, to gild it, and make it fine.

"Alfo, he fhall be bound, befide the vaulting, to make
" in frefco ten Hiftories, wherein, as fhall be given him by
" way of memorial and note, he fhall depict the life of
" the holy memory of Pope Pius, with fuch fuitable per-
" fonages, geftures, and dreffes, as may be needful and fit-
" ting to exprefs the fame, in gold, azure, ultramarine,
" enamel-blue, azure-greens, and other pleafing colours,

" fuch as may anfwer to the outlay, ftory, place, and all
" the reft.

" Alfo he fhall be bound, in refpect of the aforefaid
" figures in frefco, to retouch when dry and refinifh in
" good colours the flefh, raiment, fhades, trees, landfcapes,
" cities, atmofpheres, and borderings, and fringes.

" Alfo when he ornaments the middle lunette above
" each picture, he fhall do it in figures or whatfoever elfe he
" may choofe, or, it may be, blend it in his landfcape, or
" otherwife, as he fhall deem beft.

" Alfo he fhall be bound to make the pilafters which
" divide and furround the fpaces for the painted hiftories,
" the capitals, cornices, and bafes, in work of gold, and
" likewife the ornamentation which ferves as a bordering
" thereto, in good and fine colours, as may be beft and moft
" handfome.

" Alfo, he fhall be bound to draw all the defigns of the
" hiftories with his own hand, in cartoon and on the wall,
" to paint all the heads of the figures in frefco with his own
" hand, and to retouch them when dry, and finifh them
" to their perfection.

" Alfo he fhall be bound to make an oblong place from
" pilafter to pilafter under the hiftories, wherein fhall be
" put an epitaph (*epithaphio*) or true indication of the hiftory
" painted above, and this may be in verfe or in profe; he
" fhall alfo paint in the bafes of thefe columns and pilaf-
" ters the arms of the moft reverend Monfignore.

" And forafmuch as the aforefaid Meffer Bernardino
" hath agreed to make the vaulting of the required perfec-
" tion, and the ten pictures of fuch richnefs and excellence

"as is fitting, the moſt reverend Cardinal promiſes him one
"thouſand ducats of gold 'di camara,' in the following
"way, viz.: that firſt of all the Cardinal ſhall cauſe him
"to receive in Venice two hundred ducats of gold 'di
"'camara,' that therewith he may buy gold and neceſſary
"colours, and ſhall alſo arrange for his receiving in Peru-
"gia another hundred like ducats, to be uſed at his own
"freewill and for his own purpoſes, and to pay for the coſt
"of moving his furniture and prentices (garzoni) to Siena.
"For which three hundred ducats beforehand diſburſed,
"Meſſer Bernardino ſhall be bound to give good and ſuffi-
"cient caution that he will expend them on the work.
"And ſhould God order things otherwiſe, he ſhall make
"good and reſtore the money wholly to the ſaid Cardinal;
"it being underſtood that, if he ſhould have done any part
"of the work, a deduction *pro rata* ſhall be made. The
"reſt his executors ſhall be bound to reſtore wholly to the
"aforeſaid moſt reverend Cardinal without any exception.

"Alſo, on the completion of each picture the ſaid
"Cardinal in Siena ſhall pay fifty ducats of gold 'di
"'camara,' and ſo throughout. And when all are com-
"pletely finiſhed, then he ſhall pay him the two hundred
"remaining ducats at the end of the work and painting.

"Alſo, the ſaid moſt reverend Cardinal promiſes to the
"aforeſaid Meſſer Bernardino a dwelling at Siena rent free,
"during ſuch time as he ſhall be painting the ſaid Library,
"and to lend him (for that purpoſe) a houſe hard by the
"Cathedral: alſo, wood for ſcaffoldings, lime alſo and ſand
"enough.

"And ſince the ſaid Meſſer Bernardino, while working

"at the said Library in Siena, will need grain, wine, and
"oil; for the same price at which he might buy it from
"others, he shall be bound to take it, on account of, and
"in part payment for, the work and painting he shall do,
"from the factor of the Cardinal.

"And for the observing of the above matters the afore-
"said parties, to wit, the most reverend Monsignore, binds
"himself personally and in his goods and heirs, his move-
"ables and fixtures, present and to be, that he will wholly
"observe and keep with the aforesaid Messer Bernardino
"all the clauses and conventions herein named and ex-
"pressed, and will pay him wholly the said amount of one
"thousand gold ducats in gold 'di camara,' in the man-
"ner and at the times above specified.

"And the said Messer Bernardino, on the other part,
"promises and binds himself wholly to observe whatever
"is above contained with respect to the aforesaid most
"reverend Cardinal, and to give due guarantee for the three
"hundred ducats of gold 'di camara,' to be advanced to him
"as is stated above: binding himself also personally and in
"his goods and heirs, his moveables and fixtures, present and
"to be, that in each and every part he will wholly observe
"and do all things agreed on promised and assented to,
"undertaking all in good faith and without any reservations.

"And I, F. Cardinal of Siena aforesaid, am content,
"and do promise as above; and to assure the truth, have
"written these lines with my own hand, on the year, day,
"and month aforesaid.

"I, M. Bernardino aforesaid, am content and do
"promise, as is above contained, and to assure the truth

" have written these lines with my own hand, on the year,
" day, and month aforesaid.
" 29 June, 1502."
[Vasari (ed. G. Milanesi, Firenze, 1878), iii. p. 519.]

It strikes the reader of the above careful contract that it is an agreement with a house-decorator rather than with an artist; and in fact in that age the artist was far more usually employed to decorate than in later times: the Cardinal's eye is fixed on the splendour of the work to be done, the brightness of the colouring, the prominence and importance of the coats of arms, the brilliancy with which every inch of the surface of the library is to be covered; the originality or genius to be expended on it by the painter seems to be left in the background. He knows that he has secured an effective man; he does not trust him too far, but will pay him piece-meal, as the work is finished; he has an eye also to his own interests in detail, as is seen in the clause which compels the painter and his assistants to buy their corn and wine and oil from the prelate's factor in part-payment for their work. Not less singular is the extreme care taken to secure Pinturicchio's own handiwork; the cartoons, the actual wall-paintings, the retouching of the important parts when dry, must all be by the master himself; none of the assistants, among whom was the youthful Raphael, might take any important or responsible part in the work. And the Cardinal was doubtless quite right: Pinturicchio, though perhaps hardly a great artist or man of genius, was an admirable decorator, skilled in the technicalities of wall-painting, with its exuberance, even extravagance, of ornament and colouring. He was, too, a master of architectural drawing, and, as we see from these frescoes, very fond of introducing buildings into his work, so as to give play to his cleverness in perspective and proportion. In fact the frescoes show in the grouping and plan of action the predominance of this architectural formality; though perhaps somewhat deficient in original thought or fertility of invention, they have gold in plenty, and gilt stucco in raised work on roof and wall; they are "grotesque," as was agreed, encrusted, splendid, like the sides and vaulting of some brightly illumined cave. Much of this was done by Pinturicchio's assistants, of whom he made unsparing use; and it is characteristic of him that, though he employed more "garzoni" than any painter of his time, he nevertheless founded no school of his own; no one would venture to speak of him as Raphael's teacher. His cotemporaries at Siena declared that his execution, the technical part of his painting, was better than Perugino's, though he was far beneath that great master in sense and prudence; for he was a fellow, they added, "insipidi sermonis," a flaccid and contemptible chatterer. It is not by such men that schools of painting or anything else are formed.

Pinturicchio's true place in the Umbrian school, and his characteristic merits and defects as a painter, have been well defined by Sir Henry Layard.[1] Though we cannot rank him very high among artists, yet he is far from deserving Vasari's bitter and violent depreciation; Vasari,

[1] "The Frescoes by Bern. Pinturicchio at Spello," by A. H. Layard, M.P., Arundel Society, 1858 (v. pp. 11, 12).

indeed, can find no good thing in him, and if there are beauties in his work which he cannot help recognizing he secures his theory by always attributing them to the assistants, and more especially to Raphael. The Piccolomini Library, with all its faults, is still a great work; and it should not be forgotten that it gives us the earliest example of true historical fresco. Hitherto there had been no attempt to depict a secular history, no series of events, no portraiture on the walls of a striking biography. In such frescoes as had touched on men's lives, religious subjects had hitherto almost alone found place: they give us miracles, preachings, scriptural or saintly incidents, things all tending to edification; the historical fresco, properly so called, may be said to take its rise from the Piccolomini Library. The biographical and modern character of the work gives it a certain splendid unity of purpose, which makes the place one of the most magnificent monuments in existence, equalled perhaps only by the famous Court Church at Innspruck, built in memorial of Maximilian I., and filled with his superb and empty tomb. Yet it has great faults; the colouring is not always harmonious and satisfactory, there is a stiffness of design which is academical and disappointing, and far from being concealed by the lavish character of the decoration.

After he had signed the contract Pinturicchio wasted little time; during the autumn and winter of 1502 he made his preparations, gathered his workmen and assistants together, and removed his family to Siena; in the next spring he was hard at work in the building, beginning with the ceiling, which he appears to have completed by the autumn of 1503; for the Piccolomini coat of arms, so anxiously provided for in the contract, is surmounted by a cardinal's hat, whence it is fairly argued that it must have been finished before the painter's patron, Cardinal Francesco, placed on his brow the papal tiara; otherwise the triple crown rather than the red hat would have been depicted on the roof. Now Cardinal Francesco became Pope, as Pius III., on September 21, 1503, dying three weeks later; he may therefore have just seen the ceiling in its splendour, though the frescoes on the walls were hardly begun at the time of his death.

On his death the works were stopped for a time, and the contract being thus in a measure broken we find Pinturicchio undertaking other work, and supporting himself by his brush in other places. The late Pontiff's will, however, had expressed a wish that the library designs should be fully carried out: and his two brothers, acting as his executors, after a delay of rather more than a year, again set the work on foot. From that time, in spite of minor hindrances, it went on steadily, until after about three years' labour, in 1507 Pinturicchio completed the last of the compartments, and handed his masterpiece over to the Piccolomini family. He received the final payment under the contract in January, 1509.

I.

AENEAS . SILVIVS . PICCOLOMINEVS . NATVS . EST . PATRE SILVIO . MATRE . VICTORIA . XVIII . OCTOBR . MCCCCV . CORSIANI . IN . FVNDIS . GENTILITIIS . BASILEAM . AD . CONCILIVM . CONTENDENS . VI . TEMPESTATIS . IN . LIBYAM . PROPELLITVR.

"The person who brings you my letter is a youth of Siena, by name Æneas Silvius, of an honourable family, and very dear to me, not only because he has followed my teaching for two years, but also by reason of the keenness of his intellect, and his graceful style; his manners also are polite and cultured."

In these kindly words did the great scholar Filelfo address his friend Niccolò Arzimboldi on behalf of the needy young scion of the Piccolomini, then twenty-six years old, who was eager to make his way in the world, and to see what fame and gain his wit and scholarship might win. With the rest of the Sienese aristocracy the family of the Piccolomini had been exiled from the city after the revolution which gave the government to the popular party; they withdrew to the little village of Corsignano, where they lived long in humble estate, scarce allaying their poverty with their pride. To the representatives of the race, Silvio and Victoria, came, in 1405, a first-born son, whom they named Enea Silvio Bartolomeo;

he seems to have completely dropped the third of his
Christian names. As the parents were poor and their
family large, this eldest son, when he grew up, was sent
forth to learn the law, that he might thus have somewhat
wherewith to earn his bread. But in the strong an-
tagonism then existing between the stiff mediæval study of
the law, and the graceful and attractive classical literature,
Æneas Silvius, like Pirckheimer and Ulrich von Hutten
after him, could not long endure the uncultured style
and quibbling arguments of the lawyers; he eagerly
turned to the new fields of knowledge, in which so much
was to be done, and abandoned Institutes and Pandects
for the masterpieces of Roman letters. And so, in 1431,
we find him a zealous student of Cicero, Seneca, and
Horace, master of the art of writing neat heroics and
lyrics, with a happy knack of admirable Latin prose, and
that ingenuity, intelligence, and observation which make
the orator. As yet, however, no opportunity of exercising
these gifts had come; nor did his friend Filelfo seem able
to find him any lucrative employment.

At this time Æneas Silvius was very pale of face, and
his features were handsome, his eyes bright and merry,
though when kindled by anger they were terrible; his
well-formed mouth told of a kindly, self-indulgent nature,
a flexible and receptive temperament, with singular powers
of argument and winning persuasion. He was a man
indeed of few convictions and many impressions, quick, not
deep, kindly rather than affectionate, many-sided and
clever, not a genius or man of high nobility and elevation of character. His letters leave the impression of much

amiability, of infincerity joined, fingularly enough, with a complete franknefs as to his own conduct. It has been faid of him that " he ever arrefts our attention, though he never " wins our efteem or excites our enthufiafm ; " and this is true, in fo far as he was a man of many and varied interefts, in whom the ftrangely-interwoven civilization of the renaiffance clearly mirrored itfelf. For he was fingularly receptive and fenfitive, and worthy of the praife given him that he was " the firft modern man in hiftory . . . in him all is " genuine modern enjoyment, not a reflexion of antiquity " (Burckhardt, ii. 32), "a manifold man, in whom many " lines of thought and defire inceffantly croffed one another." This reprefentative of the age, who in more than one refpect is like his cotemporary Philip of Commines, in his contempt for the common rules of morality, in his keen infight into the world he lived with, in his love for the picturefque and the ftriking, whether in cities or on mountain fides, leaves on us a painful fenfe of infincerity, ftrangely at variance with the official praifes of the Papal hiftorian and panegyrift, Platina, who tells us that Pius II. was " truthful, a man of integrity, open, free " from all making-up or feigning." We know that as Pope he very frankly admitted his own early fhortcomings, nor did he encourage thofe falfe flatteries from others which he had formerly fo plentifully employed. He was in many ways a fingularly interefting figure ; yet, to take him all in all, we muft conclude that the more heroic and fterling qualities which make greatnefs were lacking, and that ambition, joined with felf-indulgence, filled far too large a part of the canvas of his bufy life. In ftature

Æneas was rather below the middle height, of a well-built figure and fpare habit; as he would have himfelf confeffed, this fhortnefs was the privilege of his family, indicated by their very name, the Piccolomini, the "little men."

Such a man was Æneas Silvius, when, a few months after he had received Filelfo's friendly letter, he came into communication with Domenico Capranica, Bifhop of Fermo, who was paffing through Siena on his way to the Council of Bafel. A little while before his death Martin V. had promifed the Cardinalate to Capranica, by a creation "in petto," and had, as far as he could, bound his fucceffor to announce him as Cardinal; as however his fucceffor, Eugenius IV., refufed to do this, being a friend of the Colonnas, he filled with a fenfe of wrong, and in high difcontent, was fetting off to fupport the conciliar revolt againft the Roman fee. Having heard of the gifts of young Æneas, and needing a fcholar handy with the pen, he had an interview with him, and, pleafed with his bearing, appointed him his fecretary. In his patron's fuite, Æneas fet forth at once, going on board fhip at Piombino, the port neareft to Siena; and, as fourteen years later he writes to his old comrade of thefe days, Piero da Noceto: —" We made the circuit of Corfica" . . . "a tempeft al-
" moft wrecked us on the Libyan ftrand." Still "do I
" remember well what wretched nights we paffed," the poor fecretaries, "among the feamen at Spezzia and
" Porto Venere, and how, when choked with the bilge-
" ftench from the hold, in fpite of the ftorm we chofe to
" fleep on deck rather than under cover. Together we
" faw Genoa, mother-city of the Ligurians; we climbed

"the Apennines, and after crossing the Po, visited Milan;
"we scaled the heaven-towering Alps, and crossed that
"dreadful Devil's Bridge, and Lucern Lake, and the
"Helvetian plains, until we came to Basel."

The first fresco depicts the cavalcade just setting forth for this land-journey from Genoa. The sea is behind them, still beaten with the storms which had beset their passage; and under the rain-clouds we discern the western side of the bay, covered with houses, probably just below the point on which now stands the Doria Palace with its gardens. The foreground is skilfully and beautifully filled in with figures; the complaint as to the lack of movement and life in Pinturicchio's works finds no place here; the cheerful setting forth of the storm-tossed company, glad once more to feel the solid ground beneath their feet, is well expressed by the two bright figures of gentlemen on horseback in the front; the solemnity of the churchmen in the centre of the piece is in admirable contrast with the animation of the nearer riders; nothing could be more clever than the arrangement of the piece, which is so devised that while Capranica on his mule leads the procession forwards, he is completely eclipsed by Æneas, who,—riding with easy grace a splendid white horse in the very forefront of the picture,—attracts the whole attention of the spectator. The freedom of his seat on his spirited charger contrasts well with the heavy bearing of the ecclesiastics on their plodding beasts. They have too a somewhat grim and careworn look, while Æneas is in the bloom of happy youth, a beautiful figure; his dress and jewelled cap bespeak his noble birth, and give no hint of the poor humanist-adventurer; the smile on his lips, the bright glance of his eyes, enlist our sympathy, and secure our interest in the fortunes of the hero. In his hand he daintily holds a little tablet, indicating, as delicately as possible, his position as secretary. He is seconded with much artistic skill by another and an equally graceful figure of a young man, riding a lively bay, and leading a greyhound in leash; it would be pleasant to believe that this second personage is the brother-secretary, Piero da Noceto. Under their feet spring the grasses and flowers of the early year, symbols of youth and passion; while the rainbow across the stormy sky tells that the worst is over, and that the sun again begins to shine. The whole fresco is radiant with movement, brightness, and hope. So beautiful is it, both in general effect and in the poetic management of details, that Vasari, with his usual dislike of Pinturicchio, attributes the whole of it to the hand of Raphael. It has so little of that academic formality which marks the series, that we are tempted almost to believe that it had an independent origin; yet surely it were fair, in the absence of proof to the contrary, to say that here at least Pinturicchio, though doubtless helped and inspired by his famous "garzone," did still transcend himself, and, keeping to his agreement and his duty, both conceived the piece and painted it with his own hand.

It may here be noticed in passing that in all the frescoes the line of sight is taken at about two-thirds of the way up the picture; an arrangement which, while it enables the painter more easily to fill the tall surfaces he has to deal with, places the spectator in a wrong position, and makes the whole of the architectural features appear out of perspective to one who looks at them from the floor of the Library.

This gallant setting-forth for Basel, which to the eyes of young Æneas offered so good an occasion of seeing the world and winning a position in it, was in fact a step tending directly away from the true goal of his life. Had any one told him at this time that his should be a great career as a churchman, he would have turned away in disgust. A secular, not a clerical life, was now the aim of his ambition. In a letter, written soon after his admission to deacon's orders, he tells us that a while back there was nothing he would so much have abhorred as to be counted among the clergy. For, with all his failings, he was a man of a sensitive conscience and of religious impulses; so that the restraints of the clerical calling would have galled him; the contrast between his love of pleasure and his sense of duty would have caused too painful a conflict. So now he was setting-out to enjoy the world; his moral nature had no high ideal, and though he scorned the grosser vices which prevailed in Germany, he was full of eagerness for the more refined pleasures of life, and little curious to draw too strict a line betwixt the lawful and the unlawful. There are, in all literature, few more shameless things than the letters in which he commends one of his bastard sons to his father's love and charge; he expends on the poor child the choicest common-places of Latin prose morality. And apart from this worse side of his character, Æneas was on other grounds averse to the churchman's life. The time was one of new openings for intelligent youths; and he felt in himself the qualities which ought to ensure success. He was good-looking, quick-witted, full of observation, patient, industrious; his taste was good and cultivated, and his skill in composition, so important a matter in those days, was almost unequalled. The Ciceronian writer might hope for everything, and could afford to despise the dulness or scholastic pedantry of the clergy. The career of letters opened out new vistas in every direction; and men like Æneas saw glimpses of a cultured comfortable life, in which princes and cities vied in their kindness to the learned, and almost quarrelled for the privilege of being allowed to support them. Lastly, as secretary to the aggrieved Bishop of Fermo, Æneas was committed to the anti-papal party; to him, as to his master, the claims of a General Council naturally outweighed the authority of the Papacy: Basel was a revolt against the past; the Council promised a learned reformation led by the more enlightened bishops of Europe; above all, it was an expression of that quickly-growing feeling of national life, which characterized this period, and was directly opposed to both the imperialism of the Holy Roman Empire, and the still more universal claims set up by the Papacy. To erect national churches, proclaim local independence, sway the listening world with eloquent Latin speeches of Ciceronian ring—these were the high things towards which young Piccolomini was hastening, for which he gladly left his home and fatherland.

II.

AENEAS . SILVIVS . A . BASILIENSI . CONCILIO . IN . VLTE-
RIOREM . BRITANNIAM . ORATOR . AC . SCOTIAM .
AD . REGEM . CALEXIVM . MISSVS . A . TEMPES-
TATE . IN . NOVERGIAM . PVLSVS . ET . PER .
BRITANNIAM . REGIOS . SPECVLATORES . ELVDENS .
BASILEAM . REVERTITVR.

It was not likely that the Piccolomini frefcoes would give much prominence to the Council of Bafel, confidering its ftrong anti-papal tendencies; and even the one notice of that affembly, contained in the above infcription, is hiftorically incorrect. For Æneas Silvius was not defpatched by the Council to Scotland, nor did he fet forth from Bafel. It was from Arras, whither he had accompanied his then employer, Cardinal Albergata, to the famous Congrefs of 1435, that Æneas ftarted for the Britifh Ifles. It is true that Albergata had been the reprefentative of the Council at the Congrefs, and had contributed much to the fuccefs of the negotiations there carried on; it is alfo probable that the miffion to James I. of Scotland was clofely connected with the peace made between France and Burgundy, and was, fo far, an attempt to forward the general policy of the Conciliar fathers. Still, in fpite of this, Æneas was no ambaffador from that body, nor does he appear to have carried with him their inftructions. He was fent over, in fact, by his master the Cardinal of Santa Croce, and special care seems to have been taken to divest his embassage of all appearance of being an important affair.

We may pass lightly over the life of Æneas while he was acting as a useful scholar and secretary at Basel. During this period he was servant to many masters, and tells us with a kind of pride that he had managed the correspondence of three cardinals and three bishops. Capranica, his first patron, soon became too poor to be able to support a secretary, and dismissed him; he was then taken up by Bishop Nicodemus of Freisingen, a member of the great house of the Scala, in whose suite he made his first journey to Frankfort; from him he passed on to Bartholomeo, Bishop of Novara. While with him he came into communication with both the scandalous Filippo Maria, the Visconti tyrant of Milan, whom he did not hesitate to laud with venal eloquence, and with Piccinino, the famous condottiere, whom he visited in order to lay plans for a dark plot against the person of Pope Eugenius IV., in 1435. In these unwholesome matters Æneas seems to have played the part of go-between: nor in later days did he show regret, or even resentment against the Bishop of Novara, who led him into great peril at this time; for intrigue, with its natural risks and chances, was really dear to him, and he trod lightly enough the perilous paths which might bring him to fortune. After his connection with this dangerous master was over, he fortunately found employment under Niccolò d'Albergata, Cardinal of Santa Croce, the most capable and influential man at Basel. And when the peace of Arras changed the balance of European politics, and caufed great feeling at the Court of Henry VI. of England, who threatened immediate war againſt the new confederates, it became defirable that troubles fhould, if poffible, be made for the Englifh King, fo as to hinder him from endeavouring to break up the newly-made continental peace. It was, therefore, thought well that an envoy fhould be forthwith fent to James I. of Scotland, in order to perfuade him to crofs, or at leaft to menace, the Border. And whom fhould they send? The envoy muft be perfuafive, able, refolute, and fufficiently accredited; yet not fo diftinguifhed as to attract the hoftile attention of the Englifh Court, or furnifhed with fuch definite inftructions as might, in cafe of his feizure, lead to unpleafant confequences to his mafters. There was no man at Arras who feemed to anfwer to thefe conditions better than Æneas Silvius: he had already proved his eloquence; his ftyle was beyond blame; he could be trufted to do what he was told; his induftry as well as his courage had undergone full proof; and as fecretary to the famous Cardinal of Santa Croce, he would carry weight at the Scottifh Court, while, as he had neither office nor title, it was hoped that his apparent infignificance would fecure him from too much attention. It was given out that the fecretary was being fent to James I. to reconcile a certain Scottifh prelate to that prince; or that he was going in the name of the Council and the Pope to beg for the liberation of fome perfonage held captive in Scotland. To allay fufpicion, it was thought good that he fhould avoid the long fea paffage, and attempt to pafs through England to Edinburgh. He accordingly croffed from Calais to Dover, and so through Kent to London. Here, in spite of all precautions, his further advance was stopped; and he had to retrace his steps to Dover: but not before his observant eyes, as he tells us, had been "pleased with the sight of "swarming wealthy London, and Paul's high fane and the "marvellous royal tombs (at Westminster), and Thames, "which seems to run more swiftly up than down (for to "the Italian a tidal river also was a marvel), and the "bridge which is a town in itself, and the village in which "fame says that men are born with tails, and, most note-"worthy of all, the golden mausoleum of St. Thomas of "Canterbury, all besprent with diamonds, pearls, carbuncles, "before which they deem it sacrilege to offer anything "less valuable than silver." The tail-producing town was Strood near Rochester, which legend had confused with Stroud in Gloucestershire. The story runs that when St. Augustine was passing through the West of England, he preached to the men of Stroud; and they, instead of humbly listening, made sport of him and his followers, by fastening fishes' tails to their backs: when the Saint discovered the practical joke, in his wrath he prayed that they and their luckless posterity for ever might be born with tails. This unpleasant distinction was transferred by common rumour from Gloucestershire to Kent; and thus Æneas, passing through the little town on the Medway, was told the marvel; which, like a prudent and modern man, he reports as he had heard it, without giving it any credence.

From Dover Æneas returned to the continent, passing through the famous entrepôt of Bruges to Sluys, "where is "the moft crowded harbour in all the Weft," whence he fet fail direct for the Firth of Forth. Again was his voyage unfortunate; ftormy weather from the fouthward drove him up to the Norwegian coaft, and in the wildeft time of winter he was out at fea twelve days before his ftruggling captain could land him at the port of Leith. In his fear Æneas had vowed a pilgrimage; and, directly he reached land, haftened to fulfil it, by going barefoot over fnow and ice fome ten miles to the fhrine of "our Lady of the White Kirk" in Haddingtonfhire; he was fo much exhaufted, and had fuffered fo feverely in his feet, that he had to be carried back to Edinburgh in a litter. To this painful pilgrimage he attributed in after life his frequent attacks of gout, and that infirmity of the feet which was urged againft him by his opponents at the time of his election to the papal throne.

At Edinburgh he was admitted to that interview with James I. of Scotland which forms the fubject of the fecond frefco. It is in fome refpects one of the leaft fuccefsful of Pinturicchio's efforts; for it is thoroughly unreal, and wears a peculiarly ftiff and academic look. There is no animation in the figure of Æneas, pleading as orator, nor does he ftand forth in the picture with fufficient prominence; the byftanders, who wear fancy dreffes, by no means after the Scottifh pattern, are but flightly interefted by his eloquence; King James is dignified, and the one important figure of the piece. The painter has evidently taken far more pleafure in the decoration than in the living figures; the beautiful cinque-cento arches and roof pertaining to a building never yet feen in Scotland, and very unlike Holyrood, the admirable perspective of floor and throne-steps, the pleasing landscape seen behind the royal seat, are perfectly successful as wall-ornament. But Edinburgh knew no such audience-hall; the towers of the city in the background are purely imaginary; nor are the hills and water in the least like the Firth of Forth, which they are supposed to represent; the interview took place in the dead of winter; yet Pinturicchio has his trees in full leaf, while a summer brightness floods the scene. The general effect of the colouring of this compartment is fresh and good, if we can only forget its want of truthfulness.

Though Æneas assures us that " he obtained from King " James everything for which he had come begging," he means that he had been successful in the pretexts of his embassy, and that the disgraced or imprisoned prelate was restored to favour; of the real object of the mission we hear no more. James was unwilling to create troubles for himself with England, and declared himself neutral, offering to make alliance with the parties to the Arras agreement with a view to peace only, and not for war; farther he would not go. So soon as this was quite clear, Æneas bade him farewell, receiving rich presents and money for his travelling charges; and, deeming any risk better than another long sea voyage, passed in disguise through England to Dover, and so back again to Basel. He has left in his Commentaries the most graphic account of this, which was one of the most eventful portions of his life. His keen eyes took note of all; we see that the Scots of his day were not unlike those of modern times; he praises and is allured by the comeliness of the blue-eyed women, shivers at the scant

clothing of the men, is much interested and amazed to see that when in winter the half-naked poor folk came to beg for bread, they received, in spite of the Biblical precept, a stone, and went off well contented with the gift; for in that land, he says, " they have a singular kind of sul-
" phurous stone, which is burnt instead of wood, whereof
" they have none." It is clear that the pits about Edinburgh were worked in his time, and that a winter distribution of coals to the needy was as well understood then as now. Little as may have been the political success of this mission to Scotland, we owe to it a most vivid picture of these islands as they appeared to an observant foreigner in the first half of the fifteenth century.

III.

HIC . AENEAS . A . FOELICE . V . ANTIPAPA . LEGATVS . AD . FEDERICVM . III . CAESAREM . MISSVS . LAVREA . CORONA . DONATVR . ET . INTER . AMICOS . EIVS . AC . SECRETARIVS . ANNVMERATVR . ET . PRAEFICITVR.

Some little time before his journey to Scotland, Æneas Silvius had accompanied his patron, the Cardinal of Santa Croce, to Ripaille, near Thonon, on the southern shore of Lake Leman, where the hermit-prince Amadeus of Savoy had comfortably established his little court. Scarcely a year before he had laid down his sceptre as Duke of Savoy, though he still retained the title, and continued to a considerable extent to take part in the actual government of the duchy. Under the hermit's garb the old man cloaked an ambitious spirit and luxurious tastes; the religious exercises and good living practised and enjoyed by Charles V. at Juste were not more strongly contrasted than were the hermit's dress with the easy manners of the court at Ripaille. But while honest Piero da Noceto, Æneas' fellow-secretary, saw at once through the transparent disguise, and wrote with charcoal on the wall, in Cicero's words, that "totius in-"justitiæ nulla capitalior est quam eorum, qui, cum "maxime fallunt, id agunt ut viri boni esse videantur" (De Offic., i. 13), the pliant Æneas did not choose to lift

Fresco III. 27

the cloak which covered fo great hypocrify, and from this point the career of Piero lay apart from that of his lefs fcrupulous comrade, whofe flexible code of honour led him, through many ftraits, at laft to the fummit of his ambition. For Æneas flattered the hermit with fuch fuccefs that he was invited to enter his fervice; and, as his pofition at Bafel was growing doubtful, while the leading men drew quietly away, and advancement from the Conciliar party became daily lefs probable, he hailed his appointment as fecretary to Amadeus with delight; to be at the right hand of the new anti-pope—Amadeus was elected Pope by the Council in 1439, and affumed the name of Felix V.—feemed to him to be a great ftroke of good fortune. The election of Felix, however, turned out to be fatal to the Council, and Æneas foon recognized the fact, taking precautions and prudent meafures accordingly; his pofition as " Cancellifta " in the little anti-papal court proved after all to be but a precarious preferment.

During this period Æneas fpent his leifure, of which he had no fmall amount, in literary purfuits. In the language of the time a man who followed Cicero's ftyle and efchewed the fchoolmen, who preferred artiftic compofition to logical exactitude, and drew infpiration from the Latin claffics, was ftyled a poet, whether he wrote in verfe or in profe; Cicero himfelf, in spite of his execrable hexameters, was the prince of poets, and Æneas, at Bafel, had been recognized as a poet on the ftrength of his admirable ftyle; he had alfo fpent no little time on actual verfe compofition; academic elegiacs, fatires, epiftles, worked on claffical models, and tinged with their prevalent immorality, seemed to give him a second claim to poetic honours. Above all, he painfully achieved a long Latin poem of some two thousand lines, entitled "Nymphilexis," which his friends seem to have regarded as a supreme effort of his genius. In it, as elsewhere, were apparent the loose ideas of the young man on moral questions; his private career at Basel and at the German Court was as discreditable as the apologies he thought well to offer for it in his old age.

During this period, in 1440, Frederick, Duke of Styria and Carinthia, head of the Hapsburg house, had been elected King of the Romans, and chosen Emperor with the title of Frederick III. Destined to be for half a century head of the Holy Roman Empire, it may seem strange that Frederick is so little known to posterity. He ruled through a great part of the Renaissance-period, and, though very feeble as a statesman and soldier, had the tastes and sympathies of a cultivated prince. No man had a better eye for fine jewels and stones, or more love for a well-tilled garden; he tried to give the somewhat backward German court a more literary tone. Accordingly, when Æneas Silvius came with the ambassador from Basel to the Diet at Frankfort, in 1442, and was commended to him by some leading prelates as a great master of fine Italian learning, urbanity, and style, the young German King (as the Emperor elect was properly styled previously to his coronation) was pleased at the thought of securing so much bright culture for his court, and made such handsome offers to the secretary as proved quite irresistible. He proposed to make him one of the Imperial secretaries, and also to confer on him the high, if vague dignity of Poet Laureate. Æneas readily accepted both the office and the honour; for "afterwards," he tells us, "when things were 'changed, and all abandoned Felix, refusing to recognize 'him as Pope, I, too, betook myself to Frederick the 'Cæsar; for I did not wish at once to cross over from side to side;" he did not see his way clearly to the feet of Pope Eugenius, for the transition would have been far too abrupt, and the half-starved secretary had few friends at the Roman court; he therefore caught at the opportunity of attaching himself to the neutral Germans, and to the service of one who was both a lover of letters and head of the Western world.

Though not unknown in Italy, where each prince claimed the right of conferring the laurel wreath on some learned man of his little court, where Petrarch and Dante, after his death, had been made Poets Laureate, and where the Emperor Sigismond had crowned Antonio Beccadelli at Siena in 1433, still the honour had not yet been heard of in ruder Germany. It seems to have held the place of an extraordinary and honorary degree, as it were a doctorate in arts, a special mark of literary excellence, tenable only by one happy holder at a time. If the right to confer it were conceded to each prince who might wish to have one special model of elegant scholarship at his court, there might possibly be several poets laureate at one time in different places; if, on the other hand, the head of the Holy Roman Empire were to claim it for himself alone, as now seemed probable, then the honour would be enhanced both by the dignity of the giver, and by the fact that it was tenable by only one person in the world. No wonder then that to be crowned Poet Laureate by imperial hands was regarded as a very high honour; no wonder that Æneas Silvius henceforward, till the Papacy made him superior even to this, sedulously signed himself " Poeta " in all his letters. Like his successor in the same honour, Ulrich von Hutten, he thought scorn of those degrees which indicated knowledge of the laws, and prided himself on a distinction which raised him to the highest rank among the Humanists. The diploma which declares him Poet Laureate is dated Frankfort, 27 July, 1442; it gave him the rights of an academic master of the liberal arts, authorized him to publish, read, expound, discuss, all poesy, enabled him to wear a gold-embroidered robe, with fitting ornaments.

The investiture of Æneas as Poet Laureate by Frederick III. at Frankfort forms the subject of the third fresco. He kneels, in a flowing gown, though not in that splendid robe which should betoken hereafter his new dignity, at his patron's feet; his figure and fine features are full of graceful repose. The grouping of the crowd around is sufficiently varied, though the company hardly shows much interest in the ceremony. Some of the figures are beautiful; there is a tale that the handsome boy in the right foreground of the picture (reckoning right and left by the hands of the spectator) was intended for the youthful Raphael; as this is also said of two figures in other frescoes, it may be taken for what it is worth. Pinturicchio may not improbably have, consciously or not, copied the manner and appearance of one of the most beautiful youths of his day, taking him more or less definitely as a model. The

background is one of those conventional pieces of architecture which evidently gave Pinturicchio great pleasure;
it is a fine piece of perspective work in spite of its im-
possibility as an actual building. But who can explain the
meaning of the groups in the distance? Why should a
man be stabbing a woman on the roof? and why in the
sky does a bird of prey attack a screaming goose? Does it
represent the imperial eagle swooping down on ignorance,
according to the adage, "Aquila non captat muscas,"
which was used of the great German bird? It is perhaps
worthy of note that, as if to mark the absolute neutrality
of Germany in the great question of the day, there is not
in all the crowd, not even among the courtiers by the
throne, a single ecclesiastic.

IV.

AENEAS . A . FEDERICO . III . IMP . LEGATVS . AD . EVGE-
NIVM . IIII . MISSVS . NON . SOLVM . EI . RECON-
CILIATVS . EST . SED . HIPODIACONVS . ET . SECRE-
TARIVS . MOX . TERGESTINVS . DEINDE . SENEN .
ANTISTES . CREATVS.

The Laurel Crown symbolized the transfer of the allegiance of Æneas from Felix V. to Frederick III.; yet the wary secretary did not deem it prudent to make the change till he had first applied to his late master for permission so to better his fortunes. In this he followed one chief rule of his life, which was to make no enemies among great or small; and he seems in this case to have succeeded in deserting the falling anti-pope without offending him. He doubtless pointed out that he could be serviceable to him with the German King, of whose recognition Felix as yet did not despair. And indeed for a time Æneas did not altogether sever himself from old connexions; for, though he says that " I now repented me of these their follies," he made no parade of his penitence so long as Frederick seemed likely to wed Margaret of Savoy, widow of Louis of Anjou and daughter of Felix. Nor did the visit of Frederick to Basel and the Conciliar fathers appear to him to be the right moment to show his sorrow for their errors. When, however, the marriage scheme fell through, and it became clear that Frederick would not go over to the anti-pope's side, he thought it high time to declare against the Conciliar party and its plans, and to begin in good earnest his skilful passage " from opposition through neutrality to the " Curial side."

These were also the weariest and most unhappy days of his life. The Foreign Office of Frederick III. was the home of dulness; the fellow-clerks of the new Italian secretary disliked him at once for his cleverness and for his vices; his subtle intellect, refined tastes, even his keen interest in the world around him, contrasted too much with their deadness of mind, love of routine, stuporous honesty; the Germans with their coarse tastes and commonplace amusements and gross immoralities disliked the manner of their comrade's life. Though still a layman, he had no intention of putting an inconvenient wife between himself and the chances of clerical preferment, should it seem well for him to embark on that career. A life of cynical licence was, in his view, little bar to the priesthood; a wife would have been a fatal obstacle. Yet he found small solace in his practices and amusements; his letters at this period are full of gloom; the " misery of " courtiers," of which he now wrote, a favourite theme with authors who both lack independence and smart under patronage, is described in his most eloquent manner; he tells us of poverty and neglect, dulness, ill will, a career apparently at an end, which has led him downwards at last to the drudgery of a half-starved clerk's stool. Still, things brightened somewhat when, a little later, he succeeded in winning the powerful support and friendship of Gaspar

Schlick, the German Chancellor, the man who well understood the problems of the time, and gave to German politics that direction which led to the reconciliation of Christendom, the restoration of unity, and ultimately the rise of Æneas to the papal throne. Schlick represented the wealthy burgher-party in the state; he was the "new man" the like of whom could be found in many lands, and whom princes gladly used to check the feudal aristocracy; he was the man of all others fitted to appreciate the abilities and devotion of Æneas: for the clever Italian would aid him to manage the slower Germans, and might be trusted to have nothing in common with them in either feelings or interests.

We have in that singular "Vision of Fortune" which he declares that he beheld in the year 1444, a proof of his restlessness and ambition at this time; it was also during this period that he addressed a remarkable letter to his old friend Piero da Noceto. "I serve a prince," he says, "who, as "you know, belongs to neither party, and who, holding "the middle course, desires the reunion of all. It is not "seemly that the servant should desire anything save that "which the master desires. . . . If God grants this union, "better times will come for both of us; but when this "will be, I cannot tell. In the meantime I will insinuate "myself into the King's good graces, will hearken to the "King, follow the King. What he wills, that will I: "I will never oppose him, nor interfere beyond my office. ". . . If they say yes, I will say yes; if they say no, my "no shall echo theirs." Here is no high ideal, or voice of a man of principle: let us see how the echoes of this period come back to us from him when he is no longer the struggling secretary, but the supreme Pontiff on St. Peter's seat. In his bull condemning his own works (dated 26 April, 1463), he refers to this time with open frankness: "like a "young bird from the nest, ignorant and lacking skill, we "came to Basel. . . . Our own writings pleased us then, "after the manner of poets, who recite their works; in the "ingenuous time of youth we were troubled with few "doubts, and were guided by those who were wiser and "older than ourselves. But when the Roman King re-"fused to recognize Felix V., it suited us to pass on to the "neutral party, in order that among them we might have "greater freedom to hear the truth; and, if we had to yield, "that we might not have to go over at once from one "extreme to the other."

This, then, was the position of Æneas in these years; he balanced between the parties, watching the signs of the times, and carefully taking advantage of every turn and change which might prove to be in his favour. His great patron Schlick was strongly inclined towards the side of Pope Eugenius, who lately, in September, 1443, had ventured to return to Rome. Month by month the prospects of Felix darkened; the Germans began to feel that neutrality might last too long; and finally, the threatening Turk could no more be kept out of sight. The battle of Varna (10th November, 1444), in which King Wladislas and Cardinal Cesarini met their tragic fate, left all Europe open towards the East: everything seemed to point towards reconciliation and reunion in the West.

At the very beginning of 1445 Æneas was sent by

Frederick III. to communicate to Pope Eugenius the views of the third or neutral party; they propofed that their neutrality fhould laft one year longer, during which time a general Council fhould meet at Conftance or Augfburg, or fome Danubian city, to confider and fecure the liberties of the German Church. Rome and Bafel were both invited to take part in this great affembly. While the Conciliar fathers, aware of their weaknefs, and afraid of leaving the fafe fhelter of the walls of Basel, refufed to fend envoys to fuch a council, Æneas fet forth, with his mafter's wifhes fully underftood, for Rome. Though ftill but a fecretary, from this moment he becomes a perfonage in European hiftory; to him more than to any man is due the fuccefsful healing of the fchifm of the Weft; from this time forward he deals with high thoughts of European policy; he rifes to the theme, and acquits himfelf with tact and graceful clevernefs; it is perhaps his beft time, bringing out the better fide of his character, and giving play to his fpecial gifts; he feems to have fully appreciated the greatnefs of the iffues at ftake. We become aware that there are guiding lines in his mind: the defire of the unity of the Church, and the wifh for a combined effort to ftem the forward movement of the Turks. His journey into Italy, undertaken in winter, was in itfelf no fmall teft of refolution and endurance; he encountered torrents of rain in the upland country, and found all the bridges broken in the Carinthian Alps. For three days, guided by peafants, he had to "fcale moft high and tracklefs mountains, and pre-"cipitous fnow-clad rocks." And if the thought of Italy beyond rejoiced him, he muft alfo have felt much doubt as to his reception at his journey's end. How could he, mouthpiece of conciliar eloquence at Basel, secretary afterwards to the falling anti-pope, expect to be welcome to Eugenius? Still, he somehow struggled through, going down to his beloved Siena before venturing to Rome; there his kinsfolk begged him with tears not to rush into the presence of one so fierce and unforgiving as the Pope. But Æneas knew better; if Eugenius could detach Frederick completely from the Basel fathers, and persuade him and Germany to abandon their neutrality, the schism must come to an end; and the envoy was well aware that under these circumstances he was safe enough. He also by this time had secured for himself influential friends in the Papal Curia, and had in reality little reason to dread the venture, though it afterwards pleased him to fancy himself a hero taking his life in his hand for duty's sake. "I told my "parents, that I had undertaken this embassy, and would "carry it out to a prosperous end, or perish in the "attempt."

As was no doubt foreseen, his personal reconciliation with the Pope was not long delayed, or clogged with any difficult conditions; the ceremony forms the subject of the fourth fresco. Still wearing his layman dress and long hair, Æneas kneels before Eugenius, and humbly kisses his foot; of all the compositions it is perhaps the most formal. The lines, whether of the architecture or of the groups, all converge on the central figure of the Pope, which is dignified and simple; the various tints of green on the baldachino and in the papal robes form a fine piece of delicate colouring. In the foreground sit two figures, said to be portraits of the Cardinals of Como and Amiens, warm friends of the secretary-envoy; in the background, through the arch at the pope's right hand, we see Æneas again kneeling, this time apparently to receive investiture as a cardinal; on the other hand is a little piece of landscape with unimportant figures moving through it.

The reconciliation once effected, Æneas became the centre of a great chain of negotiations; he had now made the difficult step, and had safely passed from neutrality to the papal side; the highest promotion seemed at last within his reach. Now, like his friend Gaspar Schlick, he undertook secretly to undermine, in favour of the Papacy, the neutrality of Germany, and to win the allegiance of the princes with the smallest possible concessions from the pope in return. Deftly he played his double part as open envoy of Frederick and secret agent of Eugenius; it was work for which he had a natural aptitude, strengthened by long and careful training. Though the task was difficult, and might well end in failure, it had the special advantage that it opened out rich vistas of promotion and plenty. For both pope and emperor had good things to give, and Æneas hungered much after such rewards for his services. He had already, though still a layman, held more than one piece of church preferment, the provostship of St. Lorenzo at Milan, given him by the duke, and a little Alpine parish worth sixty gold pieces yearly. But wealth and advancement clearly depended now on his abandoning the lay estate for the clerical calling; his personal dislike to the priesthood, and the unchecked licence of his life were already toning down under the

mellowing influence of years; he found his inclinations no longer at variance with his interests; "formerly," he writes to Piero da Noceto, "I had taken care not to en-
"tangle myself in holy orders, for I dreaded continence,
"which, however laudable, is more likely to be praised in
"word than followed in deed, and is more fitting to a
"philosopher than a poet; but now," he adds, "I have
"passed from the worship of Venus to that of Bacchus,"
which deity he largely praises, and seems to think that he has taken an upward step; he has become, he says, more staid in manner, and has quite changed the direction of his studies. At Basel he had worked hard at Horace, Virgil, Ovid; in Germany, he had turned to Aristotle, reading the Politics in Aretino's Latin rendering; and now, lastly, he had bought a noble Latin Bible, to the study of which he had given not a little time. And so, he says, he is quite ready for the tonsure, which a while before he would have loathed; he is prepared to cast away all thought of worldly advancement, especially as his new profession opens brighter prospects; he is far from concealing his mo-
tives: he sees benefices, a bishop's mitre, and wealthy pre-
ferments, all before him. And so, early in 1446, he is subdeacon, then deacon, and, within eighteen months, Frederick has named him Bishop of Triest. Now, however, great changes threatened him; he had all but con-
cluded with much skill and readiness the negotiations with which he was entrusted, having brought a large part of Germany back to Rome, and having good hopes of the rest, when, in February, 1447, Pope Eugenius died, and Nicolas V., who looked with no friendly eye on shifty

Æneas, ascended the pontifical throne. Having just at this time secured his nomination to the see of Trieft, he was fain to withdraw from the diplomatic tangle to the duties of his diocese. The antagonists against whom Eugenius had struggled so long survived him but a short time; in April, 1449, Felix V. quietly withdrew from his untenable position, and before the end of that year the Council of Basel had breathed its last. The fall of Gaspar Schlick in 1448, and his death in 1449, cut away all the support the new Bishop of Trieft seemed to enjoy, and for a time his bright hopes passed under eclipse.

V.

AENEAS . FEDERICO . III . IMP . LEONORAM . SPONSAM . EXHIBET . ET . PVELLAE . LAVDIS . AC . REGVM . LVSITANORVM . COMPLECTITVR.

On October 24, 1449, Æneas Silvius was named Bishop of Siena, and very thankfully he left his exile in Germany to return to his well-loved Italy. Though the republican city dreaded the effects which might follow from the rise of so able a member of the house of the Piccolomini, she still welcomed him heartily home, and was flattered by the honour done to one of her own sons. For two years, however, Æneas had little chance of settling down; he had to negotiate between the Pope and Frederick III. on the great question of the imperial coronation; he was sent as ambassador hither and thither, especially into Bohemia, where he was an eye-witness of the ferment of Hussite opinions and political agitation which made that "inland island" so interesting in the history of the age. All eastern Europe was disturbed; Hungary, Bohemia, and Austria seemed likely to fall away from Frederick's government; he pursued the phantom of the imperial dignity, at the risk of his authority over his own people. At the same time that the negotiations were going on respecting the crown, Æneas Silvius was called on to undertake another, and perhaps a more congenial task.

He was to hold himself in readiness to welcome to Italy Leonora of Portugal, the affianced bride of Frederick, who was expected to land in time to accompany him to Rome for the coronation. Accordingly in October, 1451, Æneas went down to Siena, whither, it was reported, Frederick would shortly follow. The tidings threw the jealous city into the uttermost alarm; no one knew what the Bishop might be intending; they expected a restoration of the old noble families by the intervention of the King. Æneas was flouted in the streets, threats and rumours of assassination circulated, and he thought it best to await the Infanta elsewhere. So he went down to Telamone, where she was expected to land, and waited there wearily, the weather being wintry, for two months. At last, in February, 1452, he learnt that the Portuguese ships had put in at Leghorn: thither he repaired, and after some punctilious wrangling with her escort, set out with her for Siena. Meanwhile Frederick had also come down to the same place, and on the 24th of February, 1452, hearing of her approach, set out with a splendid procession to bring her in. In the front were a hundred citizens clad in scarlet and samite; then Duke Albert of Austria, with a following of over a thousand knights; then the young King Ladislas of Hungary and Bohemia; then, duly guarded, the precious relics of the city; lastly, the clergy in their ranks. Frederick himself awaited her just outside the Camullia gate, accompanied by two cardinals, and his retinue. When the bride came in sight Frederick leapt from his horse, and hastened to meet her. He was rejoiced to see how young she was and fair.

Fresco V.

The moment of their first meeting is the scene chosen for the fifth fresco, which is, on the whole, the most lively and animated of the series. The grace and beauty of the piece, with its fine colouring and harmonious variety, have led Vasari to declare that this fresco, as well as the first, as being beyond Pinturicchio's level, was entirely the work of the youthful Raphael. There seems to be no sure foundation for this opinion. In this fresco, as in the first, Æneas, though not the important personage of the scene, still stands out as the central figure of the piece; as he delivers up the young bride to her lord, his benign face and episcopal mitre are more prominent than the dress and features of the King. Grouped around the Infanta are the ladies of her company, behind them the two cardinals. On the other side stands Ladislas of Hungary, in the foreground, with his back towards us, and Duke Albert of Austria just behind the King. In the middle of the piece rises, by a pardonable anachronism, the marble column afterwards set up on the spot, and behind it are two tall trees to symbolize the meeting of the bridal pair; the one a straight and lofty plane tree, the other a graceful fruit-bearing palm; the stems, which spring without tapering from the buttresses of their roots up to their high branching heads, show that Pinturicchio did look at the things he painted, and was not always content with conventional work. Behind the tree trunks stands the Camullia gate, and beyond, the towers, cathedral, and city walls of Siena. The spirited horses of the two companies, ranged on either side, add greatly to the fire and animation of the composition.

VI.

ÆNEAS . SENEN . ANTISTES . AD . CALISTVM . III . ORATOR
. A . FEDERICO . IMP . III . MISSVS . PONT . AD . BELLVM .
. ASIATICVM . ARMAT . ET . PATRVM . PRINCIPVMQ .
. OMNIVM . ROGATIONE . CARD . EFFICITVR.

WHEN, a week later, the bridal pair were on their way to Rome for the coronation, as the cavalcade paufed on the brow of the Ciminian hill, not far from Bolfena, and for the firft time looked down on the valley of the Tiber, Frederick called Aeneas to his fide, and faid to him, "Look "now—we go up to Rome: methinks I fee thee a car- "dinal, and in truth thy fortunes will not tarry there, thou "fhalt climb yet higher; St. Peter's chair awaits thee; "look not down on me, when thou haft reached that "pinnacle of honour." "I think not on the Pontificate,— "nay, not even on the Cardinalate," was the Bifhop's modeft reply,—a reply fcarcely in the fpirit of truth; for from this time he ftrove manfully for the red hat: when, fome years later, he was nominated cardinal, he affures us that no man had ever entered the Sacred College with fuch mighty efforts, or in face of fuch great difficulties.

Partly from a real intereft in the fubject, partly from its opportunities as a theme for the orator, partly becaufe it introduced him to the princes of Europe, and enabled him to oblige both Pope and Emperor, Æneas now took up the Turkish question, and made all Europe ring with his eloquence. It was a common ground on which the churchman and the scholar could dilate; and when, in 1453, the news of the fall of Constantinople slowly spread through the world, and all felt that while they had been playing with the danger it had fallen on them, then Æneas became the mouthpiece of the alarm. Under his fervid eloquence princes and churchmen seemed to be really moved, and he appears to have believed that a new crusade was beginning which should thrust the Moslem back across the Bosphorus. He travelled through Germany, incessant and unwearied, enjoying, it seemed, the equal confidence of Emperor and Pope. To Nicolas V., though officially he was bound to feel horror at the loss of Constantinople, the question was not so alarming as to Frederick; the Danubian frontier of Germany was more threatened than the Italian shores. Nicolas had also two sources of comfort; the Patriarch, the most important rival to Rome, had been smitten hard, and the dispersion of the learned from the East enabled him, so eager a man of letters, to gather into his library treasures of infinite worth, and to see settling in Italy many chief teachers and learned men. Nor were the services rendered by Æneas sufficient to do away with the dislike with which Nicolas regarded him: the Bishop's endeavours, the Emperor's demands, were alike vain; for Nicolas, though he had vaguely promised him the hat, never included him among the cardinals of his creation.

On his death in 1455, after a long and close struggle

in the Conclave, Alonso da Borja (Calixtus III.) was elected Pope; an old man, much respected, but infirm and unequal to the task. He spent most part of his days in bed, allowed little light and no air to enter the palace, and let himself be ruled completely by his "nephews." In his first creation of cardinals he named three youths, two of them his kinsfolk, and one of these the well-known Roderigo Lançol, on whom the Pope conferred his own family name of Borja, afterwards Alexander VI. To these worthies Æneas speedily attached himself; and when sent by Frederick to the new Pope as Imperial Envoy touching the Obedience, he seized the opportunity of abandoning that kind and easy-going master. Then it was that, after twenty-three years of busy and unhappy exile, in which he had pined not a little for the south, he at last ventured to bid farewell to Germany. Hitherto the Sacred College had been against him, and he had never dared the risks of losing the support and consideration he enjoyed as being friend and adviser to Frederick, the one Italian powerful in Germany. He had been, he tells us, up to this time a man without a true home; "omne solum," he cried, "forti patria "est"—he would rather live in comfort in Germany than starve in Italy; now however that things were changed at Rome he hesitated no longer, but abandoned his old protector, and entered on the direct road towards greatness at the papal court. From the outset of his dealings with Calixtus he threw away all thought of duty towards Frederick, all feeling for the liberties and rights of Germany; he and his colleague tendered the Obedience to the new Pope without any conditions, and coldly betrayed their trust. The one hing as to which the Pope fhowed eagernefs,—and this, perhaps, rather from what it might bring in than from any true earneftnefs,—was the projected Turkifh war, with a view to which the help of Æneas was well worth having. Accordingly, when the Bifhop of Siena returned from what feemed a fuccefsful embaffy to Naples, the Pope on December 18, 1456, againft the bitter oppofition of the College, named him, with five others, cardinal. He took the title of Cardinal Prefbyter of Santa Sabina, though, as he kept his bifhopric, he is ufually ftyled the Cardinal of Siena. " Never," he writes, " did cardinals enter the College with " greater effort. Ruft had fo clogged the hinges (a play " on the word cardinal) that the door refufed to move, nay " even ftrove to clofe itfelf. Pope Calixtus had need to ufe " the battering-ram and every kind of warlike implement, " ere he could force the way."

The fixth frefco gives us the inveftiture of the new Cardinal in the Pontifical Chapel. One of the moft quiet of the compofitions, it has dignity and fine colouring ; the cinque-cento ornamentation of the altar is ftriking, and, as ufual, the architectural drawing excellent. Pinturicchio's tafte for mere adornment has, here as elfewhere, led to too free ufe of raifed gold work, and the decorator rather ftands before the artift. The number of Cardinals prefent is very fmall ; perhaps it is intended purpofely to indicate the illwill with which the majority of the College, which was at this time unufually fmall, regarded the advancement of Æneas ; they were by no means too eager to welcome him as one of themfelves ; he brought neither wealth, nor high character, nor exalted birth ; and they above all feared his singular cleverness. In the foreground stand two Greek patriarchs or prelates, who by their presence testify satisfaction at the elevation of one who was the recognized champion of their shattered cause: they seem to promise a fresh union of Christendom, East and West joining for mutual help and defence in presence of the terrible figure of Mahomet II.

VII.

CALISTO . MORTVO . AENEAS . CARDINALIS . SENEN . ACCLA-
MATIONE . PATRVM . APERTISQVE . SVFFRAGIIS .
PONTIFEX . DELIGITVR . ET . PIVS . II . NOMI-
NATVR.

Men told, after Æneas Silvius became Pope, how his mother, just before his birth, had dreamed significant dreams, and how as a child he had been elected pope by his playfellows with mock solemnities. These things, in themselves trifles, had little influence on the first forty years of his life, during which long period he showed no taste for a clerical career. When, however, he had once begun his rapid, if difficult and encumbered, advance in that direction, he left no stone unturned, and neglected no precaution which might smooth his upward path. Patiently he continued to do his uncongenial work in Germany, so long as the imperial court could help him; he did not face the intrigues of the Curia till he was sure of a group of friends, who would not bring up against him his poverty, his infirm gait, his earlier career and hostile activity at Basel, his service under a discredited antipope, his Germanic interests and long attachment to the imperial party. Even after he had entered the Sacred College he was surrounded by enemies, who refused to be reconciled, and shunned his pleasant converse, and hated his keen intelligence. Still, as the highest prize of all was now before him, he set himself to calculate chances, to improve such advantages as he enjoyed, to reduce, as far as he could, the obstinate resistance of his ill-wishers. He had in his favour his supple wit, the support of the Spanish party, headed by the Borjas, and lastly the fact that he was an Italian, who, on the strength of his family names, Æneas and Silvius, had ventured to give himself out as of ancient Roman descent. On the other hand he had to face the hostility of the French cardinals and of some of the Italians. He had no high connections, nor was he a member of one of those families which had struck their roots deep in the soil of the Roman Curia. He therefore determined to attach himself closely to the papal nephews, and to try at the same time to accumulate wealth, without which a cardinal's chances were but poor. We find him now connected,—and little to his credit,—with Roderigo Borja, who for ability, beauty of manners, want of moral character, and greed of gain to support his extravagances, was already notable at the papal court.

This connection brings us to the meanest and most discreditable period of the life of Æneas; he made with Roderigo a scandalous compact, which reveals to us the dark side of life in the Curia ; they agreed on a plan for a joint hunt for vacant benefices. Æneas paints himself and his friend as two unclean creatures gloating over dead prelates ; Borja carrying on his rapacious work up and down the states of the church, while Æneas kept keen watch at Rome. "In the matter of benefices," he writes to his friend, "I am here to take heed for thee and for me. But " we are ever being misled by false rumours. The fellow,

Fresco VII.

lately reported dead at Nuremberg, has juſt arrived here, found and well, and I had to give him breakfaſt. The Biſhop of Toul, who, we were told, was dead at Neuſtadt, has come back in ſplendid health. Still (in ſpite of ſuch ſad diſappointments) I will keep attentive watch for anything that may really fall in." For thus did Piccolomini hope to amaſs uſeful wealth, which might befriend him when the next papal vacancy occurred. He alſo became patron for Hungary, and chief man in all attempts to ſet going a Turkiſh war: for in theſe things, too, ſomething might be made. No wonder if in theſe days he became an eloquent defender of curial abuſes; the abuſes were to his profit, while his defence of them raiſed his popularity in the papal court. Nor could any man have been more zealous in making friends and appeaſing foes: his behaviour was a pattern of courtly ſkill, ſo clever, amiable, flattering; he was the friend, nay, even the follower and diſciple, of the moſt oppoſite men; the pleaſant manners of the Italian gentleman, who had ſeen the ways, the courts, and cities of many lands, now ſtood him in good ſtead: from being at the outſet the moſt improbable of candidates for St. Peter's chair, he ſoon was felt to be " papabile."

And ſo when, in Auguſt, 1458, Calixtus III. died, though the Cardinal of Siena had worn the purple leſs than twenty months, he ſoon came to the front. He has left us a moſt ſtriking account of the incidents of the election which now took place. There were at Rome only eighteen cardinals; twelve votes would therefore make a Pope. After the firſt ſcrutiny it became clear that the choice lay between Eſtouteville, Cardinal Archbiſhop of Rouen, a wealthy and ambitious member of the houſe of Bourbon, and the Cardinal of Siena: for Æneas received five votes and was evidently ſupported by a ſtrong party. The French Cardinal had his wealth at his back; Æneas muſt truſt to his cleverneſs and ſome good friends. There were waverers among the eight votes which had been ſcattered; how were theſe to go? The French party urged that Æneas was poor and gouty, and that the dignity of the pontifical throne demanded health and wealth. Nor did they ſtop, Æneas tells us, at arguments; money was freely uſed, promiſes paſſed about in plenty; Eſtouteville's friends held a ſecret meeting by night "in latrinis," in the back-courts, and it was ſaid that he had gained over eleven voices to his ſide;—could he but add one more, he was Pope. But this twelfth voice Eſtouteville never got; at midnight Calandrini, one of the waverers, went to the cell in which Æneas was placidly ſleeping, woke him, and urged him by a thouſand conſiderations to abandon the unequal ſtruggle; it would be his wiſeſt courſe to come to terms with the poſſeſſor of eleven votes, to win the credit of making him Pope, and to wait for another vacancy. Æneas, however, did not think his chances deſperate, and refuſed to give way. A freſh ſtruggle now began in the middle of the night; the Italians beſet the waverers, urging their danger under a French Pope, the advantage of having an Italian, and appealed to their fears and cupidity with ſuch ſucceſs, that next morning at the critical ſcrutiny affairs took an entirely new turn. It was a ſtrange ſcene, told by Æneas with vivid power; we see it as freshly as if it had happened yesterday. Three cardinals, one of whom was the Cardinal of Rouen himself, were deputed, as usual, to take charge of the chalice in which the votes were deposited. The others sat in their stalls, pale and trembling with eagerness and anxiety. As Æneas came forward to deposit his slip, Estouteville could not contain himself,—for the voting was little to his mind,—and he addressed the Cardinal of Siena in these words: " Now, Æneas, let me be beholden to " thee;" to which, with ironical humility, not forgetful of the bitter opposition he had met with from his rival, he replied, " What! do even you then really commend your- " self to such a worm as I?" and placed his vote in the chalice. The names were read out as usual; and the Cardinal of Rouen declared that Æneas had eight votes, and himself six. In the midst of subdued excitement, his counting was challenged; several cardinals, who had marked down the votes as they were called, declared that nine had given their names to the Cardinal of Siena; and this was found to be true. There were now only three scattered votes out of the eighteen cardinals; if these three chose to declare for Æneas, he was Pope. In indescribable emotion it was agreed to try the " way of access," to see if any cardinal would now accede to either candidate. Long the whole conclave sat in silence; the slightest rustle of a robe, the turn of a head, the movement of a foot, sent a thrill of anxiety round the whole circle. At last the fine figure of Roderigo Borja was seen to rise, and amidst breathless stillness he, in the usual form, declared that he acceded to the Cardinal of Siena; his voice, says Æneas, was "a sword in the heart of the Cardinal of Rouen." Another pause ensued; two of the friends of Estouteville slipped out, so as to defer the election; no one, however, rose to follow them; and, after a while, their courage failed, and they silently returned to their seats. Then Cardinal Tebaldo also acceded to the Cardinal of Siena, and gave him the eleventh vote; immediately afterwards Cardinal Colonna, though vehemently held back and urged by Cardinal Estouteville himself, rose in his place and said, "And I too accede to "the Sienese, and make him Pope." Then all resistance, as usual, disappeared; the unanimous vote followed; and thus, at the age of fifty-three, Æneas Silvius Piccolomini attained the summit of his ambition. The Roman crowd outside hurried, according to ancient custom, to ransack the house of the new-made pontiff, and as Æneas was known to be poor, they conveniently had a variance as to whether it was the "Sienese" or the "Genoese" who had been elected; and, for fear of any mistake, they plundered the houses of both.

The new pontiff, who chose the title of Pius II., probably in allusion to his first name and Virgil's "Sum "pius Æneas," was crowned with all solemnity, and with the wonted street-riot, on September 3, 1458. The seventh fresco seizes that part of his procession in which, borne aloft under a baldachino which bore his coat of arms, a blue cross on a white field, and in the cross five golden half-moons, together with the pontifical insignia, he is stopped on his way, according to ancient usage, by the Master of the Ceremonies, who, kneeling before him, kindles on the tip of a reed a little tow steeped in spirit: as the brief bright flame shoots up and dies away, the official solemnly says: "Sancte Pater, sic transit gloria "mundi." He is to the Pope as the skeleton at Egyptian feasts, or the slave behind the triumphing general, a reminder of the fleeting character of the highest honours. Pius looks calmly down on the ceremony, as with hand uplifted he blesses the crowd around: his face is sad and pale, already old: travel, anxieties, ill health have told on him. The two Orientals in the foreground are there to testify to those hopes of union and resistance to the Turk, which were to be the main guiding lines of the new Pope's brief pontificate.

VIII.

PIVS . II . PONT . MAX . A . LVDOVICO . MANTVANORVM .
PRINCIPE . CLASSE . IN . NAVMACHIAE . SPECIEM .
EXCEPTVS . VI . CALENDAS . JVNIAS . MANTVAM .
AD . INDICTVM . DE . EXPEDITIONE . IN . TVRCOS .
CONVENTVM . INGREDITVR .

Two great aims characterize the life of Pius II.; his efforts for ecclesiastical unity, by restoring Germany to the Roman obedience, which were successful in the main; and his attempt to unite Christendom in a crusade against the Turks, which proved in the end a wretched failure. On the former effort rests the true title of Æneas to honour; the latter, in which he was no doubt sincere, has given him his reputation, by bringing him to an unhappy death, at the moment when his efforts had been proved completely unavailing. In earlier times Pius must have seen how little enthusiasm survived in Europe; he knew that the Turkish war was, to Pope and prince alike, little more than an easy way of raising money; he saw fleets and armies, gathered in name against the Turk, turned against Christians and used as instruments of lawless ambition. Yet, for all this, he seems not to have despaired, but ever hoped to lead the Christian world against the Infidel.

No sooner was Æneas established as Pope than he began to move the world for the purpose nearest his heart:

the embassies of the powers, bringing the obedience of the princes, were opportunities for pressing on his object; he proposed a congress in northern Italy, at which the Emperor, Philip of Burgundy, the ambassadors of Venice, the Hungarian and Bohemian princes, and, in a word, representatives of all Christian powers, might concert their measures. Pius himself left Rome early in 1459, passing through Perugia, and visiting his birth-place, Corsignano, which he raised by a decree to the rank of a city; he changed its name to Pienza, after himself, and undertook to build in the little village a stately cathedral. Thence he went to Siena, where he met with his first serious disappointment; for Philip of Burgundy, that "great Duke of the West," sent messages to say that he might be hindered from appearing at the congress. Nevertheless Pius, leaving Siena, passed by way of Florence to Mantua, where the congress was to be held. Here fresh disappointments awaited him: he had invited almost every prince; the Emperor, the German dukes and princes, the Kings of Hungary, France, England, Castile, Portugal, Arragon, the Dukes of Burgundy and Brittany, and, in fact, all lords of name and strength; from Italy he expected the Venetians, who were most nearly threatened by the Turks, as well as the representatives of all the chief cities. Yet on the appointed day not one prince, and scarcely an envoy, had arrived; Pius seemed alone in his defiance of the Turkish power,—a high position from which the heroic might easily slip into the ridiculous. Long he waited, and they would not come; as summer wore away, the envoys of the distressed Eastern Christians appeared, in ample numbers, praying for help;

but of those who should have replied with means and men
small indeed was the tale. The streets were bright with
unwonted Eastern dresses, but men-at-arms and knights
were few: even the Sacred College itself showed little zeal.
At last, two months after the appointed day, came in a
brilliant embassy from Philip of Burgundy, which was received with thankful joy by the Pope; his enthusiasm
they soon damped by showing that they and their lord were
more eager for private gain than earnest in behalf of public
objects. The two Venetian envoys also declared that if
united Europe would go, the Signoria would furnish ships to
transport the Crusaders; they refused to pledge the Republic
to separate action. Francesco Sforza presently appeared in
person, though he provided little motive force; the Polish
ambassadors were far more anxious to complain of the
Teutsch Ritters than to help forward the crusade. It was
not till near the end of September that the congress was
opened by a great speech from Pius, who declared that, in
spite of age and manifold infirmities, he would in person lead the expedition. It was, however, plain enough
that the congress was dropping into the position of a
purely Italian conference, liable at any moment to be
diverted to the private and petty aims of little princes, who
might choose to come and air their grievances. Before
the year ended, a more European character was given
to the congress by the arrival of the French envoys and
of Sigismund of Austria, who also had private ends to gain.
The business now advanced, however lamely. Pius know-
ing that the Emperor would name Albert of Brandenburg
commander-in-chief in his stead, determined to confer on

Fresco VIII.

him a classical name; and after considering whether he should style him Hector or Achilles, chose finally the latter name, remembering that Hector's fate might be of evil omen for the crusade. On January 14, 1460, war was at last formally declared against the Sultan. It was now time the congress should be closed; it had lingered on more than eight months, and Pius was perhaps the only person who did not confess it a failure, or at least, who kept up appearances to the end.

The eighth Fresco represents Pius II. directing the deliberations of the congress. In the foreground are the Eastern Christians, the suppliants; in front of the table, which is strewn with books and writings, stands a person of distinction, the Greek Patriarch as some say; he holds close and eager discussion with the Pope: behind the disputants stand a crowd of clergy and others, no doubt also representing the powers who appealed for help. On the Pope's right hand, within a low screen, sit five cardinals, indicating by their scanty numbers the small interest taken by the Sacred College; behind these, and beyond the screen, are princes and abbots, whose faces show more indifference than eagerness: through the archway of the cinque-cento hall we see a charming landscape, which seems, at some expense of geographical correctness, to represent the southern end of the Lake of Garda. The scene is completely tranquil, and rather deficient in life; there is no such enthusiastic outburst as that of Clermont, to which Pius had alluded in his opening speech.

IX.

PIVS . PONT . MAX . CATHARINAM . SENEN . OB . INNVMERA . EIVS . MIRACVLA . INTER . DIVAS . RETTVLIT.

On his return from the congress, Pius II. seemed to have forgotten all his crusading ardour. He did not hurry back to Rome; in those days Rome was a most uneasy home for a Pope, and, like others before him, Pius knew that the ground beneath his feet would be mined. Rome ever yearned for a Republic, and the first step towards that end would be the ejection of Pope and Papal Court: thus we learn from Pius himself that at this time " a Catilinarian gang," a knot of young gentlefolk, under one Tiburzio, had conspired to overthrow the priestly rule. Not till after an absence of twenty months did the Pope venture again into the Eternal City, and take steps to crush the conspiracy. Far more pleasant to him was it to linger in his own Sienese country, than to plunge into the risks and intrigues of Roman affairs. And these days were among the happiest of his life; though busy as ever, writing or dictating or giving interviews, or trying to disentangle knotted broils, he still had time to indulge his love for art and for a country life; so that he often seemed at first sight to play only the easy part of an idle and cultivated gentleman. His was a rare taste for what was picturesque and beautiful, with a fine enthusiasm for classical antiquity. Campanus assures us that he beguiled the weariness of the road to Mantua by turning aside to trace the remains of the labyrinth at Chiusi, by visiting Virgil's Mantuan farm, and by taking note of whatever was venerable or curious along his route. He published an edict for the preservation of ancient monuments; he loved hill-walks, which gave him noble distant views; he would gladly take his food beside some cool spring in the uplands, under a whispering cork tree. Near Siena he delighted himself with landscape-gardening, and planted a hill-side with the pine, cypress, ilex, and bay, with paths beneath the shade, rising by easy steps to well-chosen resting-places. To everything he brought a keen, inquiring mind, a cheerful, patient spirit. With the peasants in his path he chatted about their local interests and heard their legends with delight; he loved to talk, and to hear a pleasant joke with " free and festive converse, passing into moderate jest:" his amiable character, which prevailed even over the racking pains of his infirmities, won for him hearty friends, and bore him safely through many a trouble. Above all, he rejoiced to honour those of his own country, advancing his kinsfolk, adorning Siena, new building Corsignano: his partiality for his own family made him a great nepotist; his "nephews" received whatever he could seize for them; his highest pleasure seemed to be the restoration of his family to its position and earlier wealth. In all this there was no crusading enthusiasm: Pius appeared to be an easy Pope, whose pontificate would pass by without any action of mark; he would be reckoned among the cultured Pontiffs of the Renaissance, and no more.

Even when he was asked to decide between the rival

claims of three holy Virgins for the honour of canonization, his home partialities decided the queſtion for him. The three were Roſa of Viterbo, Franceſca of Rome, and Catherine of Siena; it muſt, however, be allowed that hiſtory has completely ratified his choice of Catherine on other and better grounds than that of a narrow local patriotiſm. She came of burgher parentage, being born at Siena in 1347, and entered young into the ſiſterhood of St. Dominic de Pœnitentia. There ſhe became famous for ſaintlineſs and for the revelations vouchſafed to her; and in the ſchiſm of the Urbaniſts and Clementines, threw her great influence into the ſcale on behalf of the Italian party. In the midſt of her half-deſpairing followers and worſhippers ſhe died in 1380. Her writings are pure and graceful, filled with a bright religious feeling; ſhe is the favourite ſubject of a whole company of painters,[1] who have depicted her, after the opinion of the day, as the ſpouſe of Chriſt: her fame ſpread wide for power of wonder-working, and when it was announced that ſhe was the choſen of the Pontiff, all Italy rejoiced.

On June 29, 1461, Pius II. publiſhed the Bull for her canonization, and with his own hand compoſed and wrote out the office for her day; nor did he fail to make a Latin poem to her praiſe. He alſo "commanded that a "high and well-appointed balcony ſhould be erected in St. "Peter's, whence, after a diſcourſe on her virtues, he might "proceed to her ſolemn canonization."

[1] A freſco painted by Gianantonio Bazzi in S. Domenico at Siena, repreſenting the Extaſy of St. Catherine after receiving the Stigmata, was publiſhed in chromo-lithography by the Arundel Society in 1867.

The fresco which represents this ceremony is in some respects one of the most interesting of the series; for although there is not much movement in it, what action there is is thoroughly dignified and suitable to the subject, and in the foreground groups are several important portraits. The composition is sharply divided into an upper and a lower compartment, and the effigy of St. Catherine, taken by Pinturicchio from her monument in the Church of S. Maria sopra Minerva at Rome, forms both a part of the dividing line, and also the natural centrepoint of the whole work. Out of the stigma in her right hand (for St. Catherine like St. Francis had the five sacred wounds) springs the white lily of purity, which bends over and seems to veil her placid countenance. Just above, at the back of the picture, sits Pius, and pronounces the canonization; his cardinals and ministers sit or stand around. In the lower compartment all are standing; there are Dominicans, Augustinians, and other churchmen, together with a representative of that sisterhood of which St. Catherine was so great an ornament; in the front are also four very striking figures, of whom the outermost on the spectator's left hand, looking out of the picture, is said to be a likeness of Raphael; next to him stands Pinturicchio himself; then lower, with his back turned and side-face hardly seen, Andrea del Sarto: one would like to know whether the handsome young man in the middle foreground represents any member of the Piccolomini family. To his right, in the robe of a Dominican, stands Fra Bartolomeo della Porta, and just behind his head we see a female face, apparently that of one of the sisters of St. Dominic.

X.

PIVS . CVM . ANCON . EXPEDITIONE . IN . TVRCOS . ACCELERARET . EX . FEBRE . INTERIIT . CVIVS . ANIMAM . HEREMITA . CAMALDVLEN . IN . COELVM . EFFERRI . VIDIT . CORPVS . VERO . PATRVM . DECRETO . IN . VRBEM . REPORTATVM . EST.

WHEN, at Mantua, Pope Pius had declared that he would himself head the crufade, the world paid little heed to his words,—nay, even doubted his fincerity. So flowly had he travelled to the congrefs, fo leifurely had he returned, long lingering at Siena and dreading to behold the gates of Rome, that men credited him at moft with a return of his old defire to fee far lands, and to vifit the Eaft as he had long ago exhaufted the Weft. And as time went on their doubts feemed better grounded; for the Pope became entangled in the petty politics of Italy, or was bufy advancing his nephews, or liftened to the learned flatteries of a Filelfo, or fpent placid days on the beautiful hills, admiring the views, and enjoying the light talk of the circle round his chair. There was no fign of fervour in the caufe abroad, or of vigour in the home government; the Pontificate of Pius has none of that decifivenefs and boldnefs which marks the rule of a powerful and original prince. Such fums as had been gathered in by Calixtus III. for the Turk-war he wafted on needlefs generofities or in local ftrife, or paying expenses of legates and missionaries to Hungary and elsewhere; the sums which might have equipped the Crusade went to distant parts to stir up an interest which never was aroused. The Turk-tithe decreed at Mantua found delay or opposition everywhere; the great embassy from the East, led by Fra Lodovico of Bologna, a Franciscan adventurer, after making much stir, collapsed; far from securing the union of East and West, or providing a solid basis for a crusade, the whole affair was mostly a delusion, and Fra Lodovico little better than an impostor dealing in travellers' tales.

And now news of the loss of one outpost of Christendom after another echoed with hollow sound through Europe. The Morea fell into Moslem hands; Rhodes and Cyprus, once bulwarks against the East, went down before the storm; the possessions of the Venetians and Genoese were snatched away with startling rapidity; the principality of Sinope and the so-called empire of Trebizond were conquered; the heroic Scanderbeg was forced to make peace: on every side the Moslem advance seemed irresistible. Under these circumstances Pius II., perhaps despairing as to the help of Europe, essayed the trial of that weapon which had stood him in good stead in old times, his classic skill in composition. It seems incredible that he could have believed in its power over the Turk. Still, he set himself to write, in his most eloquent and beautiful style, a long letter to the Sultan, Mahomet II.; credulous Christendom appears to have heard rumours of the interest taken by this great hero in the faith of Christ; his liberality and toleration, qualities so far beyond their ken, seemed to them proofs that he must be already half convinced. And so Pius penned his famous letter to the Great Turk; he uses plentiful argument, in his best Latin manner; he points out that a little water, rightly besprent, would make Mahomet the globe's emperor, the new Constantine, Lord of East and West. Whether this strange document ever reached the Sultan we know not; no trace of any genuine reply exists: the earnest oratory of the head of Christendom was completely thrown away.

And now, the danger having overwhelmed much of Greece, Venice began to feel her threatened position; and when Pasquale Malipiero, most pacific of Doges, died in 1462, the Republic indicated a change in its foreign policy by electing Christoforo Moro in his room.

At this time Pius laid before the cardinals his resolve to undertake the holy war; old as he was and worn, he would set forth, and Christian princes seeing his example for very shame would follow in his steps. This thought henceforth occupied his mind; and, with a view to this object, he strained every nerve to persuade the unwilling Christians to make peace among themselves; he mediated between the Emperor Frederick and Matthias of Hungary; he believed that he could allay the jealousies between Louis XI. and Duke Philip of Burgundy, between France and England; he signed a league with Burgundy and Venice, according to which the Duke bound himself to take ship with the Venetians, and the Pope to join them at Ancona: the Doge himself should head the Venetian force. Early in 1464 the Republic was fighting against the Turks in the Morea; but the other Italian powers held back; even

Fresco X. 67

Philip of Burgundy broke his word and sent only a reduced force under the Bastard of Burgundy, while he himself stayed quietly at home. The Pope's contingent sank low; though the discovery of alum beds in the Papal territory near Tolfa provided some resources, which Pius regarded as God's special gift for the war, still he was unable to fulfil his promises. Just as the reluctant cardinals evaded their part, and the Signoria of Venice had to undertake for them to provide galleys, so Pius, after naming as his own contingent ten galleys and many lesser vessels, failed to equip more than three ships; and of these only two lay in the roads of Ancona when he reached that town. Even at this critical time he seemed more anxious about the recovery of his health at the baths of Petriuolo, and for the advancement of his Sienese kinsfolk, than for the preparations necessary to the expedition. His envoys, however, were to some extent successful; soldiers of fortune, whom the tranquillity of Germany had reduced to penury and, worse still, to peace, streamed in crowds over the Alps to Rome or Venice or Ancona, allured by hope of booty or love of adventure; thousands came from Spain, France, and Burgundy. When they arrived, nothing was ready for them; they were led by no captains of note, nor was any one set to take them in hand; it was a mere mob of fighting-men. Deceived and disgusted, they turned back in no happy humour: few reached their homes again; famine and pest, quarrels among themselves, the vengeance of the peasantry for ruin caused by their robberies and murders, thinned their miserable ranks, and relieved Europe from the most troublesome of her children. The crusade of Pius II. was not altogether without incidental advantages.

On June 18, 1464, while the ferment still was high, Pius solemnly took the cross in St. Peter's, "an aged man, with head of snow and trembling limbs," as he said at the altar; he declared that he thus accepted the part to which he had bound himself and to which he had invited Christendom. Now, thought he, the lay princes will for very shame no longer hold back: he hoped to find at Ancona the Doge of Venice, Sforza's sons, and help from many an Italian city; he reckoned on the Burgundians, who had already set forth; for he knew not that at that moment they were making Marseilles their Capua, while they pretended to await his orders.

Immediately after this discourse he dismissed those cardinals who were to stay behind, and set out for Ancona: the farewell of the Romans, as his barge slowly stemmed the Tiber, moved him to tears: "Farewell, Rome," he cried, "living thou shalt never see me more." Already he was stricken with fever; but he made light of it, and set forth with a resolute spirit. The way was rough; the weather parching hot; he lay in the cabin of his barge, then in his litter, as one half-dead; the sight of discontented crusaders returning from Ancona, nearer to cursing than to blessing, increased his depression; the slow journey went on with painful pauses: not till July 18, just a month after the cross-taking in St. Peter's, did Pius reach Ancona. There were still some crusaders lingering there, but the ships from Venice had not come. Worn out with waiting, the adventurers slipped away, and when at last a little fleet appeared, there were none to embark. By that time it was clear, even to Pius, that the undertaking had come to naught; he passed the weary time, racked with fever, discussing and consulting with his friends. At one moment he proposed to cross over to Durazzo, and thence to issue one more appeal for help; at another time he was resolved to go no lower than Brindisi; again, he turned his eyes on Ragusa, and wished to save that city from the Turk. Still the Venetians did not come, and his disorder deepened to a more alarming form; weakness, the long journey in the heat, the manifold disappointments and anxieties, all told on his enfeebled frame; and when at last, in the middle of August, the Doge's fleet hove in sight, it was with difficulty he could even be lifted to a window to see the long-wished-for sails.

It is clear that in this last fresco Pinturicchio has taken the artist's liberties with historic truth; for no such scene could possibly have occurred as that which he depicts. Never, after the arrival of the Venetian fleet, did the dying Pope leave his chamber, yet here we see him, borne on the shoulders of six, down at the inner harbour, while Christoforo Moro kneels at his feet on one side, and an oriental at the other. Behind the Doge is a page who holds his lord's hat, a pleasing face and figure, which has also been said to represent the youthful Raphael; behind him again are Eastern merchants: on the other side, a Levantine trader, looking straight out of the picture, and behind him a little crowd of citizens. Not one ecclesiastic, not one man-at-arms, not one prince or captain stands among the groups; no warlike fervour or religious enthufiafm gleams through the picture; all is placid, as if the Pope's vifit has aroufed no intereft, his crufade no high endeavour. His face is fad and worn; he turns his back, as though in helplefs hopeleffnefs, on all the fcene; in the inner harbour one of his galleys is flipping out to fea; we can make out the Piccolomini coat-of-arms on the round bucklers which hang from her bulwarks; out in the roads beyond, lie the Venetian fhips, with fails fet, as though but juft arriving; at the Pontiff's back ftraight and fad rifes the funereal cyprefs. A look of gloom and fadnefs fills all faces; up in the fky we fee again two ominous birds, as in the third frefco; this time a weftern hawk purfues an eaftern pheafant, or is it that the imperial eagle and the Burgundian bird are together haftening Eaftwards? The whole piece, though one of the moft pleafing of the feries, lacks real feeling; at fo touching an hour, the death-point of the hero of all the tale, the moment of final failure in the great undertaking of his life, the painter has only in mind how he may flatter the Piccolomini, and pleafe their pride, not how he may render on his canvas the really tragic character of the fcene.

For tragic it indeed became: as if finally to deftroy any heroic colouring it might have worn, the Venetians loudly expreffed their belief that the dying Pope did but feign pleafure at the arrival of their fhips, and that his illnefs was fome trifling malady, exaggerated fimply that he might efcape the neceffity of fetting forth on the great expedition. Not till he had fent his phyfician to learn the truth from thofe in attendance on the Pope, was the Doge convinced as to the grim reality of the Pontiff's illnefs, and the nearness of the end. At sunset on the twelfth of August, the Venetian ships had first been descried; about the same hour on the fourteenth, Pius II. tranquilly bade farewell to life. Thus to have died, on the point of setting forth, seemed to show that he had perished a martyr to his cause. The truth was that the crusade was a hopeless failure, and that by dying Pius escaped from great embarrassment and difficulty, and from the still more alarming risk of ridicule; so great an effort, with so small result, the ever-welcome combination for the scoffer, was at once forgotten when death stood between the baffled Pontiff and his schemes. Like many another, Pius was happy in the moment of his death; it closed an active life, which yet somewhat lacked vigour and originality, with a gleam of pathos and heroism, which seemed to give to his character a touch of greatness. Yet the whole attempt had little power and foresight; it was as if with the bows and arrows of an earlier civilization the Pope would fight against the newer forces as they attacked him. Not by reviving the old crusading heat, nor by furbishing the rusty weapons of past ages, could the world resist the Moslem dominance: the fifteenth century had seen more than one attempt to solve the problems of the time, nor was it at all unnatural that a Pope should look back towards the ages of faith; yet the advance of the future lay along fairly marked lines, and Europe, just waking to a new life, refused to listen to one who called her to resume the habits of the past. Christendom, too, was paralyzed; the older feudal governments were perishing, the new monarchies not yet established; there was no unity of thought or rule; and the Turkish power, which had these elements of strength, could fearlessly advance into the very heart of Europe. Yet this crusading failure is the noblest thing in the history of Pius II.: though neither one of the first scholars of the Renaissance, nor remarkable as an administrator, nor to be counted among great popes, nor a pattern of moral excellence, nor a saint in faith or emotion, still, almost alone in Europe, he refused to sit down tamely under the insult of a Turkish conquest of half Christendom. Almost alone, Pius tried to hinder the establishment in Europe of an alien race which has held its ground even to our own day, and which at this moment still clings with a dying grasp to the last remnants of that Empire it had already won when at Ancona the worn-out Pope laid down the burden of his life.

THE END.

CHISWICK PRESS:—C. WHITTINGHAM AND CO. TOOKS COURT, CHANCERY LANE.

www.ingramcontent.com/pod-product-compliance
Lightning Source LLC
Chambersburg PA
CBHW020237090426
42735CB00010B/1736